The Best of John Donne

Featuring:

"A Valediction Forbidding Mourning"

"Meditation 17 (For Whom the Bell Tolls and
No Man is an Island)"

"Holy Sonnet 10 (Death be not Proud)"

"Come Live with me and be my Love"
And many more!

Table of Contents

The Bait

("Come Live with me and be my Love")

Come live with me, and be my love,
And we will some new pleasures prove
Of golden sands, and crystal brooks,
With silken lines and silver hooks.

There will the river whisp'ring run
Warm'd by thy eyes, more than the sun
And there th' enamour'd fish will stay,
Begging themselves they may betray.

When thou wilt swim in that live bath,
Each fish, which every channel hath,
Will amorously to thee swim,
Gladder to catch thee, than thou him.

If thou, to be so seen, be'st loth,
By sun or moon, thou dark'nest both,
And if myself have leave to see,
I need not their light, having thee.

Let others freeze with angling reeds,
And cut their legs with shells and weeds,
Or treacherously poor fish beset,
With strangling snare, or windowy net.

Let coarse bold hands from slimy nest
The bedded fish in banks out-wrest
Or curious traitors, sleeve-silk flies,
Bewitch poor fishes' wand'ring eyes.

For thee, thou need'st no such deceit,
For thou thyself art thine own bait :
That fish, that is not catch'd thereby,
Alas! is wiser far than I.

The Indifferent

I can love both fair and brown;
Her whom abundance melts, and her whom want betrays;
Her who loves loneness best, and her who masks and plays;
Her whom the country form'd, and whom the town;
Her who believes, and her who tries;
Her who still weeps with spongy eyes,
And her who is dry cork, and never cries.
I can love her, and her, and you, and you;
I can love any, so she be not true.
Will no other vice content you?
Will it not serve your turn to do as did your mothers?
Or have you all old vices spent, and now would find out others?
Or doth a fear that men are true torment you?
O we are not, be not you so;
Let me—and do you—twenty know;
Rob me, but bind me not, and let me go.
Must I, who came to travel thorough you,
Grow your fix'd subject, because you are true?

Venus heard me sigh this song;
And by love's sweetest part, variety, she swore,
She heard not this till now; and that it should be so no more.
She went, examined, and return'd ere long,
And said, "Alas! some two or three
Poor heretics in love there be,
Which think to stablish dangerous constancy.
But I have told them, 'Since you will be true,
You shall be true to them who're false to you.'"

The Broken Heart

He is stark mad, whoever says,
   That he hath been in love an hour,
Yet not that love so soon decays,
   But that it can ten in less space devour;
Who will believe me, if I swear
That I have had the plague a year?
   Who would not laugh at me, if I should say
   I saw a flash of powder burn a day?

Ah, what a trifle is a heart,
   If once into love's hands it come!
All other griefs allow a part
   To other griefs, and ask themselves but some;
They come to us, but us love draws;
He swallows us and never chaws;
   By him, as by chain'd shot, whole ranks do die;
   He is the tyrant pike, our hearts the fry.

If 'twere not so, what did become
   Of my heart when I first saw thee?
I brought a heart into the room,
   But from the room I carried none with me.
If it had gone to thee, I know
Mine would have taught thine heart to show
   More pity unto me; but Love, alas!
   At one first blow did shiver it as glass.

Yet nothing can to nothing fall,
   Nor any place be empty quite;
Therefore I think my breast hath all
   Those pieces still, though they be not unite;
And now, as broken glasses show
A hundred lesser faces, so
   My rags of heart can like, wish, and adore,
   But after one such love, can love no more.

Break of Day

Stay, O sweet, and do not rise;
The light that shines comes from thine eyes;
The day breaks not, it is my heart,
Because that you and I must part.
   Stay, or else my joys will die,
   And perish in their infancy.

[Another by the Same Name]

("Break of Day, II")

'Tis true, 'tis day; what though it be?
O, wilt thou therefore rise from me?
Why should we rise because 'tis light?
Did we lie down because 'twas night?
Love, which in spite of darkness brought us hither,
Should in despite of light keep us together.

Light hath no tongue, but is all eye;
If it could speak as well as spy,
This were the worst that it could say,
That being well I fain would stay,
And that I loved my heart and honour so
That I would not from him, that had them, go.

Must business thee from hence remove?
O! that's the worst disease of love,
The poor, the foul, the false, love can
Admit, but not the busied man.
He which hath business, and makes love, doth do
Such wrong, as when a married man doth woo.

A Hymn to God the Father

Wilt thou forgive that sin where I begun,
  Which was my sin, though it were done before?
Wilt Thou forgive that sin through which I run,
  And do run still, though still I do deplore?
When Thou hast done, Thou hast not done;
    For I have more.

Wilt Thou forgive that sin which I have won
  Others to sin, and made my sins their door?
Wilt Thou forgive that sin which I did shun
  A year or two, but wallow'd in a score?
When Thou hast done, Thou hast not done;
    For I have more.

I have a sin of fear, that when I've spun
  My last thread, I shall perish on the shore;
But swear by Thyself that at my death Thy Son
  Shall shine as He shines now and heretofore:
And having done that, Thou hast done;
    I fear no more.

The Funeral

Whoever comes to shroud me, do not harm,
    Nor question much,
That subtle wreath of hair, which crowns my arm;
The mystery, the sign, you must not touch;
    For 'tis my outward soul,
Viceroy to that, which then to heaven being gone,
    Will leave this to control
And keep these limbs, her provinces, from dissolution.

For if the sinewy thread my brain lets fall
    Through every part
Can tie those parts, and make me one of all,
Those hairs which upward grew, and strength and art
    Have from a better brain,
Can better do 't; except she meant that I
    By this should know my pain,
As prisoners then are manacled, when they're condemn'd to die.

Whate'er she meant by it, bury it with me,
    For since I am
Love's martyr, it might breed idolatry,
If into other hands these relics came.
    As 'twas humility
To afford to it all that a soul can do,
    So 'tis some bravery,
That since you would have none of me, I bury some of you.

The Relic

When my grave is broke up again
Some second guest to entertain,
　—For graves have learn'd that woman-head,
To be to more than one a bed—
　And he that digs it, spies
A bracelet of bright hair about the bone,
　Will he not let us alone,
And think that there a loving couple lies,
Who thought that this device might be some way
To make their souls at the last busy day
Meet at this grave, and make a little stay?

　If this fall in a time, or land,
　Where mass-devotion doth command,
　Then he that digs us up will bring
　Us to the bishop or the king,
　To make us relics; then
Thou shalt be a Mary Magdalen, and I
　A something else thereby;
All women shall adore us, and some men.
And, since at such time miracles are sought,
I would have that age by this paper taught
What miracles we harmless lovers wrought.

　First we loved well and faithfully,
　Yet knew not what we loved, nor why;
　Difference of sex we never knew,
　No more than guardian angels do;
　Coming and going we
Perchance might kiss, but not between those meals;
　Our hands ne'er touch'd the seals,
Which nature, injured by late law, sets free.
These miracles we did; but now alas!
All measure, and all language, I should pass,
Should I tell what a miracle she was.

The Canonization

For God's sake hold your tongue, and let me love;
   Or chide my palsy, or my gout;
   My five gray hairs, or ruin'd fortune flout;
With wealth your state, your mind with arts improve;
     Take you a course, get you a place,
     Observe his Honour, or his Grace;
Or the king's real, or his stamp'd face
   Contemplate; what you will, approve,
   So you will let me love.

Alas! alas! who's injured by my love?
   What merchant's ships have my sighs drown'd?
   Who says my tears have overflow'd his ground?
When did my colds a forward spring remove?
     When did the heats which my veins fill
     Add one more to the plaguy bill?
Soldiers find wars, and lawyers find out still
   Litigious men, which quarrels move,
   Though she and I do love.

Call's what you will, we are made such by love;
   Call her one, me another fly,
   We're tapers too, and at our own cost die,
And we in us find th' eagle and the dove.
     The phoenix riddle hath more wit
     By us; we two being one, are it;
So, to one neutral thing both sexes fit.
   We die and rise the same, and prove
   Mysterious by this love.

We can die by it, if not live by love,
   And if unfit for tomb or hearse
   Our legend be, it will be fit for verse;
And if no piece of chronicle we prove,
     We'll build in sonnets pretty rooms;
     As well a well-wrought urn becomes
The greatest ashes, as half-acre tombs,
   And by these hymns, all shall approve

Us canonized for love;

And thus invoke us, "You, whom reverend love
  Made one another's hermitage;
  You, to whom love was peace, that now is rage;
Who did the whole world's soul contract, and drove
    Into the glasses of your eyes;
    So made such mirrors, and such spies,
That they did all to you epitomize—
  Countries, towns, courts beg from above
  A pattern of your love."

Hymn to God, My God, In my Sickness

Since I am coming to that Holy room,
    Where, with Thy choir of saints for evermore,
I shall be made Thy music; as I come
    I tune the instrument here at the door,
    And what I must do then, think here before;

Whilst my physicians by their love are grown
    Cosmographers, and I their map, who lie
Flat on this bed, that by them may be shown
    That this is my south-west discovery,
    Per fretum febris, by these straits to die;

I joy, that in these straits I see my west;
    For, though those currents yield return to none,
What shall my west hurt me? As west and east
    In all flat maps—and I am one—are one,
    So death doth touch the resurrection.

Is the Pacific sea my home? Or are
    The eastern riches? Is Jerusalem?
Anyan, and Magellan, and Gibraltar?
    All straits, and none but straits, are ways to them
    Whether where Japhet dwelt, or Cham, or Shem.

We think that Paradise and Calvary,
    Christ's cross and Adam's tree, stood in one place;
Look, Lord, and find both Adams met in me;
    As the first Adam's sweat surrounds my face,
    May the last Adam's blood my soul embrace.

So, in His purple wrapp'd, receive me, Lord;
    By these His thorns, give me His other crown;
And as to others' souls I preach'd Thy word,
    Be this my text, my sermon to mine own,
    "Therefore that He may raise, the Lord throws down."

The Primrose, Being at Montgomery Castle Upon the Hill, on which it is Situate

Upon this Primrose hill,
Where, if heaven would distil
A shower of rain, each several drop might go
To his own primrose, and grow manna so;
And where their form, and their infinity
Make a terrestrial galaxy,
As the small stars do in the sky;
I walk to find a true love; and I see
That 'tis not a mere woman, that is she,
But must or more or less than woman be.

Yet know I not, which flower
I wish; a six, or four;
For should my true-love less than woman be,
She were scarce anything; and then, should she
Be more than woman, she would get above
All thought of sex, and think to move
My heart to study her, and not to love.
Both these were monsters; since there must reside
Falsehood in woman, I could more abide,
She were by art, than nature falsified.

Live, primrose, then, and thrive
With thy true number five;
And, woman, whom this flower doth represent,
With this mysterious number be content;
Ten is the farthest number; if half ten
Belongs to each woman, then
Each woman may take half us men;
Or—if this will not serve their turn—since all
Numbers are odd, or even, and they fall
First into five, women may take us all.

The Flea

Mark but this flea, and mark in this,
How little that which thou deniest me is;
It suck'd me first, and now sucks thee,
And in this flea our two bloods mingled be.
Thou know'st that this cannot be said
A sin, nor shame, nor loss of maidenhead;
   Yet this enjoys before it woo,
   And pamper'd swells with one blood made of two;
   And this, alas! is more than we would do.

O stay, three lives in one flea spare,
Where we almost, yea, more than married are.
This flea is you and I, and this
Our marriage bed, and marriage temple is.
Though parents grudge, and you, we're met,
And cloister'd in these living walls of jet.
   Though use make you apt to kill me,
   Let not to that self-murder added be,
   And sacrilege, three sins in killing three.

Cruel and sudden, hast thou since
Purpled thy nail in blood of innocence?
Wherein could this flea guilty be,
Except in that drop which it suck'd from thee?
Yet thou triumph'st, and say'st that thou
Find'st not thyself nor me the weaker now.
'Tis true; then learn how false fears be;
Just so much honour, when thou yield'st to me,
Will waste, as this flea's death took life from thee.

The Good-Morrow

I wonder by my troth, what thou and I
Did, till we loved? were we not wean'd till then?
But suck'd on country pleasures, childishly?
Or snorted we in the Seven Sleepers' den?
'Twas so; but this, all pleasures fancies be;
If ever any beauty I did see,
Which I desired, and got, 'twas but a dream of thee.

And now good-morrow to our waking souls,
Which watch not one another out of fear;
For love all love of other sights controls,
And makes one little room an everywhere.
Let sea-discoverers to new worlds have gone;
Let maps to other, worlds on worlds have shown;
Let us possess one world; each hath one, and is one.

My face in thine eye, thine in mine appears,
And true plain hearts do in the faces rest;
Where can we find two better hemispheres
Without sharp north, without declining west?
Whatever dies, was not mix'd equally;
If our two loves be one, or thou and I
Love so alike that none can slacken, none can die.

Go and Catch a Falling Star

Go and catch a falling star,
Get with child a mandrake root,
Tell me where all past years are,
Or who cleft the devil's foot,
Teach me to hear mermaids singing,
Or to keep off envy's stinging,
      And find
      What wind
Serves to advance an honest mind.

If thou be'st born to strange sights,
Things invisible to see,
Ride ten thousand days and nights,
Till age snow white hairs on thee,
Thou, when thou return'st, wilt tell me,
All strange wonders that befell thee,
      And swear,
      No where
Lives a woman true and fair.

If thou find'st one, let me know,
Such a pilgrimage were sweet;
Yet do not, I would not go,
Though at next door we might meet,
Though she were true, when you met her,
And last, till you write your letter,
      Yet she
      Will be
False, ere I come, to two, or three.

Elegy 2: The Anagram

Marry, and love thy Flavia, for she
Hath all things, whereby others beauteous be;
For, though her eyes be small, her mouth is great;
Though they be ivory, yet her teeth be jet;
Though they be dim, yet she is light enough;
And though her harsh hair fall, her skin is tough;
What though her cheeks be yellow, her hair's red,
Give her thine, and she hath a maidenhead.
These things are beauty's elements; where these
Meet in one, that one must, as perfect, please.
If red and white, and each good quality
Be in thy wench, ne'er ask where it doth lie.
In buying things perfumed, we ask, if there
Be musk and amber in it, but not where.
Though all her parts be not in th' usual place,
She hath yet an anagram of a good face.
If we might put the letters but one way,
In that lean dearth of words, what could we say?
When by the gamut some musicians make
A perfect song, others will undertake,
By the same gamut changed, to equal it.
Things simply good can never be unfit;
She's fair as any, if all be like her;
And if none be, then she is singular.
All love is wonder; if we justly do
Account her wonderful, why not lovely too?
Love built on beauty, soon as beauty, dies;
Choose this face, changed by no deformities.
Women are all like angels; the fair be
Like those which fell to worse; but such as she,
Like to good angels, nothing can impair:
'Tis less grief to be foul, than to have been fair.
For one night's revels, silk and gold we choose,
But, in long journeys, cloth and leather use.
Beauty is barren oft; best husbands say,
There is best land, where there is foulest way.
Oh, what a sovereign plaster will she be,
If thy past sins have taught thee jealousy!

Here needs no spies, nor eunuchs; her commit
Safe to thy foes, yea, to a marmoset.
When Belgia's cities the round country drowns,
That dirty foulness guards and arms the towns,
So doth her face guard her; and so, for thee,
Which forced by business, absent oft must be,
She, whose face, like clouds, turns the day to night;
Who, mightier than the sea, makes Moors seem white;
Who, though seven years she in the stews had laid,
A nunnery durst receive, and think a maid;
And though in childbed's labour she did lie,
Midwives would swear 'twere but a tympany;
Whom, if she accuse herself, I credit less
Than witches, which impossibles confess;
One like none, and liked of none, fittest were;
For things in fashion every man will wear.

Elegy 19: To His Mistress Going to Bed

Whoever loves, if he do not propose
The right true end of love, he's one that goes
To sea for nothing but to make him sick.
Love is a bear-whelp born : if we o'er-lick
Our love, and force it new strange shapes to take,
We err, and of a lump a monster make.
Were not a calf a monster, that were grown
Faced like a man, though better than his own?
Perfection is in unity; prefer
One woman first, and then one thing in her.
I, when I value gold, may think upon
The ductileness, the application,
The wholesomeness, the ingenuity,
From rust, from soil, from fire ever free;
But if I love it, 'tis because 'tis made
By our new nature, use, the soul of trade.
    All this in women we might think upon,
—If women had them—and yet love but one.
Can men more injure women than to say
They love them for that, by which they're not they?
Makes virtue woman? must I cool my blood
Till I both be, and find one wise and good?
May barren angels love so. But if we
Make love to woman, virtue is not she,
As beauty is not, nor wealth. He that strays thus
From her to hers is more adulterous
Than if he took her maid. Search every sphere
And firmament, our Cupid is not there.
He's an infernal God, and underground
With Pluto dwells, where gold and fire abound.
Men to such gods their sacrificing coals
Did not on altars lay, but pits and holes.
Although we see celestial bodies move
Above the earth, the earth we till and love.
So we her airs contemplate, words and heart,
And virtues, but we love the centric part.
    Nor is the soul more worthy, or more fit
For love, than this, as infinite as it.

But in attaining this desired place
How much they err, that set out at the face?
The hair a forest is of ambushes,
Of springes, snares, fetters, and manacles;
The brow becalms us when 'tis smooth and plain,
And when 'tis wrinkled, shipwrecks us again;
Smooth, 'tis a paradise, where we would have
Immortal stay, but wrinkled 'tis a grave.
The nose, like to the first meridian, runs
Not 'twixt an east and west, but 'twixt two suns;
It leaves a cheek, a rosy hemisphere,
On either side, and then directs us where
Upon the islands fortunate we fall,
Not faint Canaries, but ambrosial,
Her swelling lips, to which when we are come,
We anchor there, and think ourselves at home,
For they seem all; there Sirens' songs and there
Wise Delphic oracles do fill the ear.
There, in a creek where chosen pearls do swell,
The remora, her cleaving tongue, doth dwell.
These and the glorious promontory, her chin,
O'erpast, and the straight Hellespont between
The Sestos and Abydos of her breasts,
Not of two lovers, but two loves, the nests,
Succeeds a boundless sea, but yet thine eye
Some island moles may scattered there descry;
And sailing towards her India, in that way
Shall at her fair Atlantic navel stay.
Though there the current be the pilot made,
Yet, ere thou be where thou shouldst be embay'd,
Thou shalt upon another forest set,
Where many shipwreck, and no further get.
When thou art there, consider what this chase
Misspent by thy beginning at the face.
   Rather set out below; practise thy art;
Some symmetry the foot hath with that part
Which thou dost seek, and is thy map for that,
Lovely enough to stop, but not stay at.
Least subject to disguise and change it is;
Men say the devil never can change his;
It is the emblem that hath figured

Firmness; 'tis the first part that comes to bed.
Civility we see refined; the kiss,
Which at the face began, transplanted is,
Since to the hand, since to the imperial knee,
Now at the papal foot delights to be.
If kings think that the nearer way, and do
Rise from the foot, lovers may do so too;
For, as free spheres move faster far than can
Birds, whom the air resists, so may that man
Which goes this empty and ethereal way,
Than if at beauty's elements he stay.
Rich Nature in women wisely made
Two purses, and their mouths aversely laid.
They then which to the lower tribute owe,
That way which that exchequer looks must go;
He which doth not, his error is as great,
As who by clyster gives the stomach meat.

A Valediction: of Weeping

    Let me pour forth
My tears before thy face, whilst I stay here,
For thy face coins them, and thy stamp they bear,
And by this mintage they are something worth,
    For thus they be
    Pregnant of thee;
Fruits of much grief they are, emblems of more,
When a tear falls, that thou falls which it bore,
So thou and I are nothing then, when on a diverse shore.

    On a round ball
A workman that hath copies by, can lay
An Europe, Afric, and an Asia,
And quickly make that, which was nothing, all;
    So doth each tear
    Which thee doth wear,
A globe, yea world, by that impression grow,
Till thy tears mix'd with mine do overflow
This world; by waters sent from thee, my heaven dissolved so.

    O more than moon,
Draw not up seas to drown me in thy sphere,
Weep me not dead, in thine arms, but forbear
To teach the sea what it may do too soon;
    Let not the wind
    Example find,
To do me more harm than it purposeth;
Since thou and I sigh one another's breath,
Whoe'er sighs most is cruellest, and hastes the other's death.

A Valediction Forbidding Mourning

As virtuous men pass mildly away,
   And whisper to their souls to go,
Whilst some of their sad friends do say,
   "Now his breath goes," and some say, "No."

So let us melt, and make no noise,
   No tear-floods, nor sigh-tempests move;
'Twere profanation of our joys
   To tell the laity our love.

Moving of th' earth brings harms and fears;
   Men reckon what it did, and meant;
But trepidation of the spheres,
   Though greater far, is innocent.

Dull sublunary lovers' love
   —Whose soul is sense—cannot admit
Of absence, 'cause it doth remove
   The thing which elemented it.

But we by a love so much refined,
   That ourselves know not what it is,
Inter-assurèd of the mind,
   Care less, eyes, lips and hands to miss.

Our two souls therefore, which are one,
   Though I must go, endure not yet
A breach, but an expansion,
   Like gold to aery thinness beat.

If they be two, they are two so
   As stiff twin compasses are two;
Thy soul, the fix'd foot, makes no show
   To move, but doth, if th' other do.

And though it in the centre sit,
   Yet, when the other far doth roam,
It leans, and hearkens after it,

And grows erect, as that comes home.

Such wilt thou be to me, who must,
  Like th' other foot, obliquely run;
Thy firmness makes my circle just,
  And makes me end where I begun.

Air and Angels

Twice or thrice had I loved thee,
    Before I knew thy face or name;
    So in a voice, so in a shapeless flame
Angels affect us oft, and worshipp'd be.
    Still when, to where thou wert, I came,
Some lovely glorious nothing did I see.
    But since my soul, whose child love is,
Takes limbs of flesh, and else could nothing do,
    More subtle than the parent is
Love must not be, but take a body too;
    And therefore what thou wert, and who,
      I bid Love ask, and now
That it assume thy body, I allow,
And fix itself in thy lip, eye, and brow.

Whilst thus to ballast love I thought,
    And so more steadily to have gone,
    With wares which would sink admiration,
I saw I had love's pinnace overfraught;
    Thy every hair for love to work upon
Is much too much; some fitter must be sought;
    For, nor in nothing, nor in things
Extreme, and scattering bright, can love inhere;
    Then as an angel face and wings
Of air, not pure as it, yet pure doth wear,
    So thy love may be my love's sphere;
      Just such disparity
As is 'twixt air's and angels' purity,
'Twixt women's love, and men's, will ever be.

The Triple Fool

I am two fools, I know,
 For loving, and for saying so
  In whining poetry;
But where's that wise man, that would not be I,
  If she would not deny?
Then as th' earth's inward narrow crooked lanes
 Do purge sea water's fretful salt away,
I thought, if I could draw my pains
 Through rhyme's vexation, I should them allay.
Grief brought to numbers cannot be so fierce,

For he tames it, that fetters it in verse.
 But when I have done so,
 Some man, his art and voice to show,
  Doth set and sing my pain;
And, by delighting many, frees again
  Grief, which verse did restrain.
To love and grief tribute of verse belongs,
 But not of such as pleases when 'tis read.
Both are increasèd by such songs,
 For both their triumphs so are published,
And I, which was two fools, do so grow three.
Who are a little wise, the best fools be.

The Sun Rising

Busy old fool, unruly Sun,
    Why dost thou thus,
Through windows, and through curtains, call on us?
Must to thy motions lovers' seasons run?
    Saucy pedantic wretch, go chide
    Late school-boys and sour prentices,
  Go tell court-huntsmen that the king will ride,
  Call country ants to harvest offices;
Love, all alike, no season knows nor clime,
Nor hours, days, months, which are the rags of time.

    Thy beams so reverend, and strong
    Why shouldst thou think?
I could eclipse and cloud them with a wink,
But that I would not lose her sight so long.
    If her eyes have not blinded thine,
    Look, and to-morrow late tell me,
  Whether both th' Indias of spice and mine
  Be where thou left'st them, or lie here with me.
Ask for those kings whom thou saw'st yesterday,
And thou shalt hear, "All here in one bed lay."

    She's all states, and all princes I;
    Nothing else is;
Princes do but play us; compared to this,
All honour's mimic, all wealth alchemy.
    Thou, Sun, art half as happy as we,
    In that the world's contracted thus;
  Thine age asks ease, and since thy duties be
  To warm the world, that's done in warming us.
Shine here to us, and thou art everywhere;
This bed thy center is, these walls thy sphere.

Holy Sonnet I

Thou hast made me, and shall Thy work decay?
Repair me now, for now mine end doth haste;
I run to death, and Death meets me as fast,
And all my pleasures are like yesterday.
I dare not move my dim eyes any way;
Despair behind, and Death before doth cast
Such terror, and my feeble flesh doth waste
By sin in it, which it towards hell doth weigh.
Only Thou art above, and when towards Thee
By Thy leave I can look, I rise again;
But our old subtle foe so tempteth me,
That not one hour myself I can sustain.
Thy grace may wing me to prevent his art
And thou like adamant draw mine iron heart.

Holy Sonnet II

As due by many titles I resign
Myself to thee, O God. First I was made
By Thee; and for Thee, and when I was decay'd
Thy blood bought that, the which before was Thine.
I am Thy son, made with Thyself to shine,
Thy servant, whose pains Thou hast still repaid,
Thy sheep, Thine image, and—till I betray'd
Myself—a temple of Thy Spirit divine.
Why doth the devil then usurp on me?
Why doth he steal, nay ravish, that's Thy right?
Except Thou rise and for Thine own work fight,
O! I shall soon despair, when I shall see
That Thou lovest mankind well, yet wilt not choose me,
And Satan hates me, yet is loth to lose me.

Holy Sonnet III

O! might those sighs and tears return again
Into my breast and eyes, which I have spent,
That I might in this holy discontent
Mourn with some fruit, as I have mourn'd in vain.
In mine idolatry what showers of rain
Mine eyes did waste? what griefs my heart did rent?
That sufferance was my sin, I now repent;
'Cause I did suffer, I must suffer pain.
Th' hydroptic drunkard, and night-scouting thief,
The itchy lecher, and self-tickling proud
Have the remembrance of past joys, for relief
Of coming ills. To poor me is allow'd
No ease; for long, yet vehement grief hath been
Th' effect and cause, the punishment and sin.

Holy Sonnet IV

O, my black soul, now thou art summoned
By sickness, Death's herald and champion;
Thou'rt like a pilgrim, which abroad hath done
Treason, and durst not turn to whence he's fled;
Or like a thief, which till death's doom be read,
Wisheth himself deliver'd from prison,
But damn'd and haled to execution,
Wisheth that still he might be imprisoned.
Yet grace, if thou repent, thou canst not lack;
But who shall give thee that grace to begin?
O, make thyself with holy mourning black,
And red with blushing, as thou art with sin;
Or wash thee in Christ's blood, which hath this might,
That being red, it dyes red souls to white.

Holy Sonnet V

I am a little world made cunningly
Of elements, and an angelic sprite;
But black sin hath betray'd to endless night
My world's both parts, and, O, both parts must die.
You which beyond that heaven which was most high
Have found new spheres, and of new land can write,
Pour new seas in mine eyes, that so I might
Drown my world with my weeping earnestly,
Or wash it if it must be drown'd no more.
But O, it must be burnt; alas! the fire
Of lust and envy burnt it heretofore,
And made it fouler; let their flames retire,
And burn me, O Lord, with a fiery zeal
Of Thee and Thy house, which doth in eating heal.

Holy Sonnet VI

This is my play's last scene; here heavens appoint
My pilgrimage's last mile; and my race
Idly, yet quickly run, hath this last pace;
My span's last inch, my minute's latest point;
And gluttonous Death will instantly unjoint
My body and soul, and I shall sleep a space;
But my ever-waking part shall see that face,
Whose fear already shakes my every joint.
Then, as my soul to heaven her first seat takes flight,
And earth-born body in the earth shall dwell,
So fall my sins, that all may have their right,
To where they're bred and would press me to hell.
Impute me righteous, thus purged of evil,
For thus I leave the world, the flesh, the devil.

Holy Sonnet VII

At the round earth's imagined corners blow
Your trumpets, angels, and arise, arise
From death, you numberless infinities
Of souls, and to your scattered bodies go;
All whom the flood did, and fire shall o'erthrow,
All whom war, dea[r]th, age, agues, tyrannies,
Despair, law, chance hath slain, and you, whose eyes
Shall behold God, and never taste death's woe.
But let them sleep, Lord, and me mourn a space;
For, if above all these my sins abound,
'Tis late to ask abundance of Thy grace,
When we are there. Here on this lowly ground,
Teach me how to repent, for that's as good
As if Thou hadst seal'd my pardon with Thy blood.

Holy Sonnet VIII

If faithful souls be alike glorified
As angels, then my father's soul doth see,
And adds this even to full felicity,
That valiantly I hell's wide mouth o'erstride.
But if our minds to these souls be descried
By circumstances, and by signs that be
Apparent in us not immediately,
How shall my mind's white truth by them be tried?
They see idolatrous lovers weep and mourn,
And stile blasphemous conjurers to call
On Jesu's name, and pharisaical
Dissemblers feign devotion. Then turn,
O pensive soul, to God, for He knows best
Thy grief, for He put it into my breast.

Holy Sonnet IX

If poisonous minerals, and if that tree,
Whose fruit threw death on (else immortal) us,
If lecherous goats, if serpents envious
Cannot be damn'd, alas! why should I be?
Why should intent or reason, born in me,
Make sins, else equal, in me more heinous?
And, mercy being easy, and glorious
To God, in His stern wrath why threatens He?
But who am I, that dare dispute with Thee?
O God, O! of Thine only worthy blood,
And my tears, make a heavenly Lethean flood,
And drown in it my sin's black memory.
That Thou remember them, some claim as debt;
I think it mercy if Thou wilt forget.

Holy Sonnet X ("Death be Not Proud")

Death, be not proud, though some have called thee
Mighty and dreadful, for thou art not so;
For those, whom thou think'st thou dost overthrow,
Die not, poor Death, nor yet canst thou kill me.
From rest and sleep, which but thy picture[s] be,
Much pleasure, then from thee much more must flow,
And soonest our best men with thee do go,
Rest of their bones, and soul's delivery.
Thou'rt slave to Fate, chance, kings, and desperate men,
And dost with poison, war, and sickness dwell,
And poppy, or charms can make us sleep as well,
And better than thy stroke; why swell'st thou then?
One short sleep past, we wake eternally,
And Death shall be no more; Death, thou shalt die.

Holy Sonnet XI

Spit in my face, you Jews, and pierce my side,
Buffet, and scoff, scourge, and crucify me,
For I have sinn'd, and sinne', and only He,
Who could do no iniquity, hath died.
But by my death can not be satisfied
My sins, which pass the Jews' impiety.
They kill'd once an inglorious man, but I
Crucify him daily, being now glorified.
O let me then His strange love still admire;
Kings pardon, but He bore our punishment;
And Jacob came clothed in vile harsh attire,
But to supplant, and with gainful intent;
God clothed Himself in vile man's flesh, that so
He might be weak enough to suffer woe.

Holy Sonnet XII

Why are we by all creatures waited on?
Why do the prodigal elements supply
Life and food to me, being more pure than I,
Simpler and further from corruption?
Why brook'st thou, ignorant horse, subjection?
Why dost thou, bull and boar, so sillily
Dissemble weakness, and by one man's stroke die,
Whose whole kind you might swallow and feed upon?
Weaker I am, woe's me, and worse than you;
You have not sinn'd, nor need be timorous.
But wonder at a greater, for to us
Created nature doth these things subdue;
But their Creator, whom sin, nor nature tied,
For us, His creatures, and His foes, hath died.

Holy Sonnet XIII

What if this present were the world's last night?
Mark in my heart, O soul, where thou dost dwell,
The picture of Christ crucified, and tell
Whether His countenance can thee affright.
Tears in His eyes quench the amazing light;
Blood fills his frowns, which from His pierced head fell;
And can that tongue adjudge thee unto hell,
Which pray'd forgiveness for His foes' fierce spite?
No, no; but as in my idolatry
I said to all my profane mistresses,
Beauty of pity, foulness only is
A sign of rigour; so I say to thee,
To wicked spirits are horrid shapes assign'd;
This beauteous form assures a piteous mind.

Holy Sonnet XIV

Batter my heart, three-person'd God; for you
As yet but knock; breathe, shine, and seek to mend;
That I may rise, and stand, o'erthrow me, and bend
Your force, to break, blow, burn, and make me new.
I, like an usurp'd town, to another due,
Labour to admit you, but O, to no end.
Reason, your viceroy in me, me should defend,
But is captived, and proves weak or untrue.
Yet dearly I love you, and would be loved fain,
But am betroth'd unto your enemy;
Divorce me, untie, or break that knot again,
Take me to you, imprison me, for I,
Except you enthrall me, never shall be free,
Nor ever chaste, except you ravish me.

Holy Sonnet XV

Wilt thou love God as he thee? then digest,
My soul, this wholesome meditation,
How God the Spirit, by angels waited on
In heaven, doth make His temple in thy breast.
The Father having begot a Son most blest,
And still begetting—for he ne'er begun—
Hath deign'd to choose thee by adoption,
Co-heir to His glory, and Sabbath' endless rest.
And as a robb'd man, which by search doth find
His stolen stuff sold, must lose or buy it again,
The Sun of glory came down, and was slain,
Us whom He had made, and Satan stole, to unbind.
'Twas much, that man was made like God before,
But, that God should be made like man, much more.

Holy Sonnet XVI

Father, part of His double interest
Unto Thy kingdom Thy Son gives to me;
His jointure in the knotty Trinity
He keeps, and gives to me his death's conquest.
This Lamb, whose death with life the world hath blest,
Was from the world's beginning slain, and He
Hath made two wills, which with the legacy
Of His and Thy kingdom do thy sons invest.
Yet such are these laws, that men argue yet
Whether a man those statutes can fulfil.
None doth; but thy all-healing grace and Spirit
Revive again what law and letter kill.
Thy law's abridgement, and Thy last command
Is all but love; O let this last Will stand!

Holy Sonnet XVII

Since she whom I loved hath paid her last debt
To Nature, and to hers, and my good is dead,
And her soul early into heaven ravishèd,
Wholly on heavenly things my mind is set.
Here the admiring her my mind did whet
To seek thee, God; so streams do show the head;
But though I have found thee, and thou my thirst hast fed,
A holy thirsty dropsy melts me yet.
But why should I beg more love, whenas thou
Dost woo my soul, for hers offering all thine:
And dost not only fear lest I allow
My love to saints and angels, things divine,
But in thy tender jealousy dost doubt
Lest the world, flesh, yea, devil put thee out.

Holy Sonnet XVIII

Show me, dear Christ, thy spouse so bright and clear.
What! is it she which on the other shore
Goes richly painted? or which, robbed and tore,
Laments and mourns in Germany and here?
Sleeps she a thousand, then peeps up one year?
Is she self-truth, and errs? now new, now outwore?
Doth she, and did she, and shall she evermore
On one, on seven, or on no hill appear?
Dwells she with us, or like adventuring knights
First travel we to seek, and then make love?
Betray, kind husband, thy spouse to our sights,
And let mine amorous soul court thy mild dove,
Who is most true and pleasing to thee then
When she is embraced and open to most men.

Holy Sonnet XIX

Oh, to vex me, contraries meet in one:
Inconstancy unnaturally hath begot
A constant habit; that when I would not
I change in vows, and in devotion.
As humorous is my contrition
As my profane love, and as soon forgot:
As riddlingly distempered, cold and hot,
As praying, as mute; as infinite, as none.
I durst not view heaven yesterday; and today
In prayers and flattering speeches I court God:
Tomorrow I quake with true fear of his rod.
So my devout fits come and go away
Like a fantastic ague; save that here
Those are my best days, when I shake with feare.

Meditation 17 ("For Whom the Bell Tolls" and "No Man is an Island")

From "Devotions upon Emergent Occasions" (1623), XVII: Nunc Lento Sonitu Dicunt, Morieris - "Now, this bell tolling softly for another, says to me: Thou must die."

Perchance he for whom this bell tolls may be so ill, as that he knows not it tolls for him; and perchance I may think myself so much better than I am, as that they who are about me, and see my state, may have caused it to toll for me, and I know not that.

The church is Catholic, universal, so are all her actions; all that she does belongs to all.

When she baptizes a child, that action concerns me; for that child is thereby connected to that body which is my head too, and ingrafted into that body whereof I am a member.

And when she buries a man, that action concerns me: all mankind is of one author, and is one volume; when one man dies, one chapter is not torn out of the book, but translated into a better language; and every chapter must be so translated; God employs several translators; some pieces are translated by age, some by sickness, some by war, some by justice; but God's hand is in every translation, and his hand shall bind up all our scattered leaves again for that library where every book shall lie open to one another.

As therefore the bell that rings to a sermon calls not upon the preacher only, but upon the congregation to come, so this bell calls us all; but how much more me, who am brought so near the door by this sickness.

There was a contention as far as a suit (in which both piety and dignity, religion and estimation, were mingled), which of the religious orders should ring to prayers first in the morning; and it was determined, that they should ring first that rose earliest.

If we understand aright the dignity of this bell that tolls for our evening prayer, we would be glad to make it ours by rising early, in that application, that it might be ours as well as his, whose indeed it is.

The bell doth toll for him that thinks it doth; and though it intermit again, yet from that minute that this occasion wrought upon him, he is united to God.

Who casts not up his eye to the sun when it rises? but who takes off his eye from a comet when that breaks out? Who bends not his ear to any bell which upon any occasion rings? but who can remove it from that bell which is passing a piece of himself out of this world? No man is an island, entire of itself; every man is a piece of the continent, a part of the main.

If a clod be washed away by the sea, Europe is the less, as well as if a promontory were, as well as if a manor of thy friend's or of thine own were: any man's death diminishes me, because I am involved in mankind, and therefore never send to know for whom the bell tolls; it tolls for thee.

Neither can we call this a begging of misery, or a borrowing of misery, as though we were not miserable enough of ourselves, but must fetch in more from the next house, in taking upon us the misery of our neighbours.

Truly it were an excusable covetousness if we did, for affliction is a treasure, and scarce any man hath enough of it.

No man hath affliction enough that is not matured and ripened by it, and made fit for God by that affliction.

If a man carry treasure in bullion, or in a wedge of gold, and have none coined into current money, his treasure will not defray him as he travels.

Tribulation is treasure in the nature of it, but it is not current money in the use of it, except we get nearer and nearer our home, heaven, by it.

Another man may be sick too, and sick to death, and this affliction may lie in his bowels, as gold in a mine, and be of no use to him; but this bell, that tells me of his affliction, digs out and applies that gold to me: if by this consideration of another's danger I take mine own into contemplation, and so secure myself, by making my recourse to my God, who is our only security.

The End

If you enjoyed <u>The Best of John Donne</u>, then check out the best of other poets in The Classic Poet Series, such as <u>The Best of John Keats</u>, <u>The Best of Lord Alfred Tennyson</u>, <u>The Best of Thomas Moore</u>, and many, many more!